ECTED POEMS

KT-426-718

ANDREW MOTION

Selected Poems
1976–1997

ff

faber and faber

First published in 1998
by Faber and Faber Limited
3 Queen Square London WC1N 3AU

Photoset by Wilmaset Ltd, Birkenhead, Wirral
Printed in England by Mackays of Chatham plc, Chatham, Kent

© Andrew Motion, 1998

Andrew Motion is hereby identified as author of this
work in accordance with Section 77 of the Copyright,
Designs and Patents Act 1988

A CIP record for this book
is available from the British Library

ISBN 0-571-19504-0

10 9 8 7 6 5 4

for Jan Dalley

Acknowledgements

While preparing this book I have made a number of changes to several poems.

'A Dying Race', 'In the Attic', 'Anniversaries', 'Inside and Out' and 'Leaving Belfast' first appeared in *The Pleasure Steamers* (Carcanet, Manchester, 1976).

'Independence' was first published by the Salamander Press (Edinburgh, 1981).

'The Lines, 'Anne Frank Huis', 'The Letter', 'The Great Man', 'On Dry Land', 'Bathing at Glymenopoulo' and 'From the Imperial' first appeared in *Secret Narratives* (Salamander Press, Edinburgh, 1983).

'Dangerous Play' first appeared in *Dangerous Play: Poems 1974–1984* (Salamander Press, Edinburgh, 1986, and Penguin, 1987).

'The Dancing Hippo' first appeared in *Natural Causes* (Chatto and Windus, 1987).

'Look', 'One Who Disappeared', 'A Blow to the Head', 'The Prague Milkbottle', 'Hull', 'Missing' (previously called 'Tamworth') and 'It is an Offence' first appeared in *Love in a Life* (Faber and Faber, 1991).

'Lines of Desire' first appeared in *The Price of Everything* (Faber and Faber, 1994).

'Salt Water', 'Reading the Elephant', 'The Spoilt Child', 'Dead March', 'Does That Hurt?', 'Your Postcard Came', 'Goethe in the Park', 'To Whom It May Concern', 'Tortoise', 'On the Table', 'Hey Nonny' and 'Fresh Water' first appeared in *Salt Water* (Faber and Faber, 1997).

Contents

I

A Dying Race

The less I visit, the more
I think myself back to your house
I grew up in. The lane uncurled
through candle-lit chestnuts
discovers it standing four-square,
whitewashed unnaturally clear,
as if it were shown me by lightning.

It's always the place I see,
not you. You're somewhere outside,
waving goodbye where I left you
a decade ago. I've even lost sight
of losing you now; all I can find
are the mossy steps you stood on
– a visible loneliness.

I'm living four counties away, and still
I think of you driving south each night
to the ward where your wife is living.
How long will it last?
You've made that journey six years
already, taking each broken-off day
as a present, to please her.

I can remember the fields you pass,
the derelict pill-boxes squatting
in shining plough. If I was still there,
watching your hand push back

the hair from her desperate face,
I might have discovered by now
the way love looks, its harrowing clarity.

In the Attic

Even though we know now
your clothes will never
be needed, we keep them,
upstairs in a locked trunk.

Sometimes I kneel there
touching them, trying to relive
time you wore them, to catch
the actual shape of arm and wrist.

My hands push down
between hollow, invisible sleeves,
hesitate, then take hold
and lift:

a green holiday; a red christening;
all your unfinished lives
fading through dark summers
entering my head as dust.

Anniversaries

The fourth

Anniversary weather: I drive
under a raw sunset, the road
cramped between drifts, hedges
polished into sharp crests.

I have it by heart now;
on this day in each year
no signposts point anywhere
but east into Essex,

and so to your ward,
where snow recovers tonight
the ground I first saw lost
four winters ago.

Whatever time might bring,
all my journeys take me
back to this dazzling dark:
I watch my shadow ahead

plane across open fields,
out of my reach for ever,
but setting towards your bed
to find itself waiting there.

The first

What I remember is not
your leaving, but your not
coming back – and snow
creaking in thick trees,

burying tracks preserved
in spiky grass below.
All afternoon I watched
from the kitchen window

a tap thaw in the yard,
oozing into its stiff sack,
then harden when evening
closed with ice again.

And I am still there,
seeing your horse return
alone to the open stable,
its reins dragging behind

a trail across the plough,
a blurred riddle of scars
we could not decipher then,
and cannot heal now.

The second

I had imagined it all –
your ward, your shaved head,
your crisp scab struck there
like an ornament,

but not your stillness.
Day after day I saw
my father leaning forward
to enter it, whispering

'If you can hear me now,
squeeze my hand', till snow
melted in sunlight outside
then turned to winter again

and found him waiting still,
hearing the slow hiss
of oxygen into your mask,
and always turning to say

'Yes, I felt it then',
as if repeating the lie
had gradually made it true
for him, never for you.

The third

Three years without sight,
speech, gesture, only
the shadow of clouds
shifting across your face

then blown a world away.
What sleep was that, which
light could never break?
What spellbound country

claimed you, forbidding you
even to wake for a kiss?
If it was death,
whose hands were those

warm in my own, and whose
astonishing word was it
that day when leaving
your sunlit room I heard

'Stay; stay', and watched
your eyes flick open once,
look, refuse to recognise
my own, and turn away?

The fourth

The evening falls with snow
beginning again, halving
the trees into whiteness,
driving me with it towards

the end of another year.
What will the next one bring
that this has abandoned?
You are your own survivor,

giving me back the world
I knew, without the years
we lost. Until I forget
whatever it cannot provide

I'll always arrive like this,
having no death to mourn,
but rather the life we share
nowhere beyond your room,

our love repeating itself
like snow I watch tonight,
which spins against my window
then vanishes into the dark.

The Lines

November, and the Sunday twilight fallen
dark at four – its hard unbroken rain
battering the garden. Vacantly I fill
this first weekend alone with anything –

the radio, a paperback you never read:
In 1845 200,000 navvies, 3,000 miles of line.
Lost faces lift – *a mania, a human alligator,*
shovels clinking under high midsummer sun.

The heat-haze dances meadowsweet and may,
whole cliffs collapse, and line by line
I bring your death to lonely hidden villages,
red-tiled farms, *helpless women and timid men.*

Inside and Out

Two hundred miles from home I found
the one freezing room where you live,
and that, as you said, was *Nothing,
really. Not even my own. See this?
It's Madame Dussart's funeral gown,
filling a whole drawer. Supposing
I died first, of boredom, what then?*

Then nothing again. A vacant space
where no one would see the sunlight
mark time in dust towards your bed.
As if we were ghosts of ourselves
we waited for darkness, watching it
deepen to bring us together again
like shadows, our close definition.

And shadows we stayed, or tried to,
knowing, before it fell, that night
after night would discover us still
caught in our absolute lives. If not
the room, what was there outside to blame,
hidden except when headlights below
reminded us where they travelled towards?

Vimy, Arras, Bapaume: I thought of
the brilliant signs, whitening south
through your country of maps and towns
in history. Nothing escaped itself—
not even the wind, tracing a ridge

of lost lines over the fields, always
raising the same delicate spray of graves.

They were complete societies, flickering
stones I knew by distant village names.
However I chose I remembered them,
all preserved no matter what deaths
succeeded them there, and us, who talking
each other to sleep at last heard only
their luminous silence we could not survive.

Leaving Belfast
for Craig Raine

Driving at dusk on the steep road
north to the airport, *Look back,*
you say, *The finest view of Belfast,*
and point, proud of your choice to stay.

How clear the rows of streetlamps show
which way we came. I trace them slope
by slope through marshland slipping down
to lanes, and find the roofs again,

their stern geographies of punishment
and love where silence deepens under rain.
Each sudden gust of light explains itself
as flames, but neither they, nor even

bombs redoubled on the hills tonight
can quite include me in their fear.
What does remains invisible, is lost
in curt societies whose deaths become

revenge by morning, and whose homes
are what they pity most.
I watch the moon above them, filling rooms
with cut-out politics, though whether

voices there pronounce me an intruder,
traitor, or a friend, I leave them now
as much a stranger as I came, my car
beginning on its way again, the road

a hair-line crack, a thread, a wire
I see unwound ahead through miles
of stubborn gorse, until it disappears
at last in darkness, out along the coast.

Anne Frank Huis

Even now, after twice her lifetime of grief
and anger in the very place, whoever comes
to climb these narrow stairs, discovers how
the bookcase slides aside, then walks through
shadow into sunlit rooms, can never help

but break her secrecy again. Just listening
is a kind of guilt: the Westerkirk repeats
itself outside, as if all time worked round
towards her fear, and made each stroke
die down on guarded streets. Imagine it –

three years of whispering and loneliness
and plotting, day by day, the Allied line
in Europe with a yellow chalk. What hope
she had for ordinary love and interest
survives her here, displayed above the bed

as pictures of her family; some actors;
fashions chosen by Princess Elizabeth.
And those who stoop to see them find
not only patience missing its reward,
but one enduring wish for chances

like my own: to leave as simply
as I do, and walk at ease
up dusty tree-lined avenues, or watch
a silent barge come clear of bridges
settling their reflections in the blue canal.

II

The Letter

If I remember right, his first letter.
Found where? My side-plate perhaps,
or propped on our heavy brown tea-pot.
One thing is clear – my brother leaning
across asking *Who is he?* half angry
as always that summer before enlistment.

Then alone in the sunlit yard, mother
unlocking a door to call *Up so early?*
– waving her yellow duster goodbye
in a small sinking cloud. The gate creaks
shut and there in the lane I am running
uphill, vanishing where the woodland starts.

The Ashground. A solid contour swept
through ripening wheat, and a fringe
of stippled green shading the furrow.
Now I am hardly breathing, gripping
the thin paper and reading *Write to me.*
Write to me please. I miss you. My angel.

Almost shocked, but repeating him line
by line, and watching the words jitter
under the pale spidery shadows of leaves.
How else did I leave the plane unheard
so long? But suddenly there it was –
a Messerschmitt low at the wood's edge.

What I see today is the window open,
the pilot's unguarded face somehow
closer than possible. Goggles pushed up,
a stripe of ginger moustache, and his eyes
fixed on my own while I stand
with the letter held out, my frock blowing,

before I am lost in cover again,
heading for home. He must have banked
at once, climbing steeply until his jump
and watching our simple village below –
the Downs swelling and flattening, speckled
with farms and bushy chalk-pits. By lunch

they found where he lay, the parachute
tight in its pack, and both hands spread
as if they could break the fall. I still
imagine him there exactly. His face pressed
close to the sweet-smelling grass. His legs
splayed wide in a candid unshamable V.

The Great Man

It was straight out of Conrad but true.
At midday I rounded the umpteenth turn
of the river, and there was the man himself,
surprised in the hospital yard. Just as I thought,
he was all I had never expected – far older,
no sign of the famous moustache, and the walk
a frightened scamper towards the jungle,
one hand cramming a yellow hat hard down.

He returned and was smiling, of course,
for the evening meal. *You are a journalist?*
Wonderful. Wonderful yes. And have taken a week?
To be with us? Or get here? Never you worry.
Someone will show you the hospital soon–
that is a pride and joy. If it were now,
I could not remember the clammy weight
of his hand on my shoulder more clearly,
half welcoming, half for support. Or the way
his eyes were scanning my face but staring
at someone else. Whoever it was appeared again
when he played – which was done like a maestro:
theatrical strides to the dais when supper was over,
and servants dragging his masterpiece centre-stage.

A rickety, straight-up, knee-hole, bamboo organ.
I knew about this. I had read in the books
how natives would 'gratefully leave their hearths
and listen enchanted for hours'. But I never imagined
he might have performed like a drain. He fumbled

through most of a fugue, steadfastly fixing his gaze
on the someone or something I could not see,
then the rain drowned him – beginning at sunset
like clockwork, and sullenly pounding the metal roof.

It never let up until morning. Lying in bed
I could follow a handful of patients prowling their ward
from window to window – glistening torsos and heads
as long as the power held out, and afterwards
abstract blurs. But just to be there was a cure,
everyone knew. Wasn't the doctor so gentle
he even avoided the ant which crossed his path?
How much he did for the dying, I would find out,
tagging along on his rounds with my camera poised.
Master. Master. You are a god to us. That was the woman
we found next day in the yard – the first of dozens.
She drew back the shawl from her raspberry shoulders
with almost a smile, but the doctor was shaking his head.
He prayed, which he always did, then ordered a poultice
of warm riverbank mud to be bound on her skin.

If I had said he was fake, who would have listened?
I was a stranger, and strangers were not to be trusted.
Do nothing, was all I could think. *When you are home,
then say whatever you like*. Well, here I am home today
– with my notebook and photographs spread on my desk,
and the rain which has blanketed London this morning
creasing my windows. Its whisper is scarcely a sound,
but it softens the stop-go scratching my pencil makes:
*He must have been eighty by then, but the moment
our ramshackle steamer nosed in by the jetty, there he was
striding to greet us, crushing my hand in his grip.*

On Dry Land

I lost one slipper going down,
the other surfacing. Overboard
barefooted! Think of sharks.
Think of how I hung there
treading water, dizzy, stunned
and shouting for my luggage –
shirts and trousers billowing
below me over sunken rope
and drowned unflinching heads.

And dozens still to jump. I saw
some naked, some in uniform
crawl out on deck, climb up
its tilting, polished slope,
hesitate, and leap at last.
The darkness buried them,
each hopeless figure lost
for ever with those horses
screaming as the water rose.

Days away, I woke. A corridor,
the nurses, and a voice above me
saying *Alexandria. This is Alex.*
Opposite my bed two soldiers
turned to look, then hunched
above an orange box again.
Watching where a scorpion
and scuttling small tarantula
circled on their stage of leaves.

Bathing at Glymenopoulo

Lotus eating. I can believe it:
first moment ashore the heat
whacked us – a lavish blast
and the stink of horses.
Then it was *Mister. Mister.*
Captain Mackenzie – bathing girls
round from the beach, white
towels and parasols weaving
through gun-carriages, crates
and saddlery lined on the quay,
to pelt us with flowers. *Want*
Captain Mackenzie? I give you
good times. But we rode away,
eyes front and smiling,
pursued until the Majestic gates.

Men to the grounds, officers
one to a cool high-ceilinged room –
mine with a balcony looking
down to the lake. There were pelicans
clambering carefully in and out
and in, never still, wrecking
the stagnant calm, fighting,
and shaking their throats
with a flabby rattle. Otherwise,
peace: the cedar layered
in heavy green-black slabs
and shading tents on the lawn;

the horses only a rumour,
stamping and snorting
out by the kitchen garden.

Early each morning we rode
to Christmas Hill – two hours
of dressage in dusty circuits,
then home with the sun still low.
For the rest, time was our own;
no orders, no news from France,
but delicious boredom: polo
some evenings, and long afternoons
bathing at Glymenopoulo.
Iras, I have you by heart, giggling
and stumbling up from the breakers
into my photograph, one thin hand
pressed to your cheek, your knee-
length, navy-blue costume puckered
and clinging. I singled you out

day after day after day –
to swim with, to dawdle with
arm in arm on the beach
as the sun disappeared, and later
to hear your pidgin whispers
dancing in waterfront cafés:
You not like anyone. Gentler
than other Captain Mackenzies.
You not like the others –
your lemony hair
loose and brushing my mouth,
your bracelets clinking,
and languorous slow waltzes

twirling us round and round
in the smoky half-light. *Luck,*

I told myself. *Luck;*
it will end. But the lazy days
stretched into weeks
with each one the same—
Luck; it will end—
until we were riding
one brilliant morning
as ever to Christmas Hill.
And half-way, at Kalia,
stopped at our watering place—
a date-grove fringing the pool,
and the whole platoon fanned out
in a crescent to drink.
I was dismounted, leading my horse
over sugary sand, empty-headed

and waving flies from my face
when the firing began. Ten shots,
perhaps — flips and smacks
into date trunks, and nobody hurt.
But we charged, all of us thinking
At last! Action at last!
as we wheeled through the trees
and away, drawing our swords
with stupid high-pitched yelps,
labouring on through a silver mirage-lake
then finding them waiting.
Senussi, no more than a dozen,
their gypsy silhouettes

slinking back into stones
as we breasted the rise.

The end of the world. A sheer
wall falling hundreds of feet
to a haze of yellow scrub.
I wrenched myself round, sword
dropped, head low, to a dead
teetering halt as our line
staggered, and buckled,
and broke in a clattering slide.
I can hear it again – the panicking
whinnies, shouts, and the rush
of scree where they shambled off
into space. It has taken three days
to bury them; one for the trek
to the valley floor, one to scratch
their ranks of graves, one to return.

There is little the same. At six
we have curfew now: I am writing this
after dark on my knee in the School
of Instruction grounds, in a tent.
I cannot sleep. Sirens disturb me,
groaning up from the harbour.
Those are the ships from Gallipoli,
unloading their trail of stretchers
to the Majestic, where you will be
waiting, Iras, I know, stopped
outside the gates, high-heeled
just as you were, with your hair

fluffed out after swimming:
Captain! Want Captain Mackenzie?
I give you. I give you good times.

From the Imperial

Now I am almost asleep
and the hotel is locked,
whose is this voice,
this dream companion,
dead a century ago?

He lives as I imagine –
Edward Lear,
lonely and bigongulous,
wishing he were an egg,
climbing dark stairs

towards a room like mine,
and drawing shutters tight
on powder-moonlight fallen
jiggy-jaggy in the bay.
Such silent darknesses.

Such secrecy. From night
to night he keeps himself
without a word for love,
and then sails north at last,
his boat weighted down

with cases, tables, chairs
and an upright black piano
strapped and locked on deck,
the varnish quickly warming
as it flashes back the sun.

Independence

for Alan Hollinghurst

A month home, and awake
at three expecting light.
Still half the world in darkness
to roll away – but here I am

by the window, stooping,
briskly smearing a hole
in the silvery glass.
Your father's house.

His view of sand dunes
stubbled with grass, and the sea
heavily sliding, its craters split
and slammed shut to the moon.

As I look, wind staggers
the garden lilac, then races off
distressing the whole front:
the neighbour's gate squeaking

and banging, the pub-sign
knocking its frame once, twice,
and still. But who is awake?
I glance at my bed and the sheet

thrown back, a shrunken ghost
where I slept – on the right,
making room for you still.
Making room. And there,

with no more than the thought,
you are lifting towards me again —
in silence, bringing the friends,
the lost company, servants I left.

Everyone bowed and shawled
as though it were dawn, and this
wavering grey moonlight the dust
they had churned into early mist.

*

It was dawn in fact
when my journey finished at last —
three days, three nights stop-go
in that rickety Austin, a jangling

sweep from the Punjab down
past Delhi, Agra, Kanpur, to reach
Kamaria: higgledy roofs and the sun
clear into perfect blue. I drove

along sleeping streets, wide-eyed,
still scared. But no sign of the riots —
just slogans splashed and dribbling:
Partition. No to Partition. Quit India.

What of my factory? Would it be looted
by then? Or what? The manager's voice
came back to me, nervous and jabbing:
Now we are free. No Britishers.

Now you must go – but smiling,
shaking my hand. Then I was home
with my servant running to greet me:
Yes go, sahib. It is dangerous. Go.

All I could save went with me –
one suitcase, Shakespeare, a china mug,
and the *Hindustan Times*, three days old.
I can see it now – your father's advertisement

circled in violet ink, his name the friend
of a friend of a friend. In a week,
when I stood in his white-washed hall
for my interview, early, rehearsing my lines,

you appeared. A sudden unthinking
rush from your room, from a shower,
your hair darkened with water
and plastered down, your feet bare,

and one hand pulling the throat
of your dressing-gown close,
half-hiding the freckled blush
I glimpsed, painful and raw like a burn.

*

Our first blue midwinter.
Each cavernous morning
I drove to the godown at six
stocktaking wool for an hour:

indigo, crimson, natural, gold.
Then away round the villages –
The carpet sahib. Carpets!
And trained as an engineer!

House by house I ducked
and entered those low mud rooms.
The silences! Fathers and sons
on their shiny logs,

frowning through bars of string.
The twang and rustle of wool,
and the patterns rising.
Finish how soon? More frowns,

the waggling side-to-side headshake,
Goodbye, and as evening came on
I circled back to your bungalow.
Would you be home? If I drove

from Mirzapur, east, it was over
the Ganges bridge. I would stop
midway and leaning giddily out
puzzle the drop through twilight,

then crumple a rupee note for luck
and throw it – straining to watch –
but never expecting the fall to end
on the river's lugubrious green.

*

It was our first time. We had shuffled
and clutched at Club dances, and once
after tennis I kissed you, my hand
finding the marble small of your back.

Next thing I knew it was midnight,
and I had dropped down
in the hospital garden —
your nervous, adoring commando.

So which was your room?
Third right, in your letter. *Please.*
Oh please come soon. I've been well
for at least ten days. My appendix just sits

in its jar on the window sill, staring me out.
Your shutter unstuck with a parched squeak.
Is it you? Yes. We were laughing but then
as I leant to your face, missing your mouth,

frozen, our heads drilled through
by the hard tap-tapping of footsteps.
Nurse! Quick! In there! Next thing again
I was dragging your cupboard door shut

behind me, losing myself in your clothes,
just catching your bright *No, nothing,*
thank you. Nothing. I'm fine. Good night . . .
before it was time to come back to the world

once more, and let it dissolve:
the cupboard, your room, your bed, the coat
I would rip on the wall when I scrambled home
but wear unmended for days as our secret sign.

*

Courting all that spring
to Independence – spring
and into the heat: days
I hurried to end for you.

Each late afternoon
we were side by side
at your father's bungalow,
longing for sunset, the punkah

lightly pressing us down
with its soft load of air.
He frowned. *All right –
well, supper's not yet . . .*

and we were away, squeezed
in the Austin's cracked back seat,
the windows open, our driver's face
blank as a stone in the mirror.

They were perfect,
those evening drives:
the sunlight bleary with dust,
white eucalyptus avenues,

trim, sweet-smelling fires,
and woodsmoke rising to heaven.
When will you marry me? Soon?
When you said it, you said it lazily,

pressing your mouth to my ear,
on that juddering, pot-holed road
somewhere out beyond Mirzapur.
We were late, with the engine off

at the crossing – a slender pole
waist high, and the heat still
shimmering up from the rails,
warping the air. The keeper

slipped out of his shack,
lifted the pole, listened,
and slammed it back.
What now? you said,

chafing my hand, then waited
in silence, hearing the train
chomp closer, the rails tingle,
a shrieking whistle,

and there it was. *Benares/
Lahore* on chipped plates,
windows barred, and the hollow
vanished faces of refugees.

*

Married a month and stirring slowly,
making room in our lives
for lives outside our own.
Spring brought the heat again –

day by day in my office the papers
leavened under their weights,
shaken and plucked as the punkah
whipped round in its clammy rush.

On my wall I had pinned the first
free replacement map – India,
Pakistan: the new word jagged
up through the Indus valley to end

in the mountains' lumpy bruise.
When Gandhi died, your father
traced the frontier down –
Now. Now we shall see –

and bowed his head. Next day
he was out in the villages talking,
cajoling, then back at my desk
empty-handed. *It's grief*, he said.

They won't do anything. Nothing.
You understand. You know.
He stared at my map and sighed,
gradually tracing his way

down through labyrinth-fields
and into Bombay, coming to rest
among gantries huddled in mist,
a dockside seething then clear.

*

With your father gone, his furniture
gone or stacked in the godown,
the house was ours: echoing rooms
and the spaces he left: dents in a carpet

for chairs, the crushed square of a desk.
Each night was our private game. *Listen.*
What can you hear? You would be stretched
flat out with your dress rumpled up,

holding my head to your stomach. *Anything?*
Yes. I said what you wanted. *A boxer.*
Or maybe a football player. We slept outside
that summer, wide-eyed effigies hand

in hand on the cool veranda, our hearts racing,
watching the harum star-trails shoot
away through our nets. This lasted a month.
Two months. Two and a half. And then

my trip to Delhi on business. Should you
have risked it? Was that it? Even in summer?
One thing is certain. I still cannot finish
my journey back. Here comes the taxi again,

dithering home from the station and here
I am crouching inside it, the windows down
so my eyes blur, and the house melts
with the one servant who meets me.

Where is the memsahib? The question
has fallen dead in the yard and cannot get up.
Sahib, he says, just that. The rest is the sun
in splinters. And crickets. Their crazy bowing.

*

A scar of yellow clods.
The scratchmark of some-
thing vanished. A dry scuffle.
You will wake up,

I am thinking. *Wake up!*
shutting my eyes,
my head to the earth
as if I might just

make you out underground:
your hair soaked through,
your face empty,
your bloodless mouth,

and the dress slinking back
from your bare arms
as you stretch and show me
our dead child who killed you.

*

Then everything is afterwards.
Days adrift at work, embarrassed
by those sad half-shouts
above the doodling punkah:

Can I help you, sahib?
And evenings drunk alone –
the bedroom shutters drawn,
my shadow reeling to

and fro across their slats
collapsing dresses into tea-chests,
scooping up the baby-things,
your belts, a thrown-down petticoat,

shoes, blouses from the cupboard.
So much of you to find!
Three nights, but always something
overlooked, and then a fourth,

and rain. Almost home,
I was dreaming through the yard
and stifling when it broke.
A long-drawn sizzling rip

like linen tearing,
then a pause, and then
the first big drops, distinct
and smashed in puffing spurts of dust.

Monsoon again. That night
I stretched across our bed
and drank among your last
unsorted clothes, the houselights

all turned off. No sleep,
but blankness interrupted
suddenly to find the rain
had quickened, thunder

cannoning above my roof,
the eucalyptus shimmering
and thrashed, its whole
enormous height smoking

in a constant crash.
Then blankness swimming back,
the rain retreating,
and a dream releasing me

beyond my room, my garden,
bobbing on a grey race
of water to your grave.
I scrambled deep beside you

and was dry, tugging
at your clothes, whispering
Let go. Come back to me.
Let go. Come back to me. Let go.

*

How many days? Two? Three?
I sank from the world,
half-sleeping or dreaming awake,
with the rain a steady downpour

seething to rot me through.
When next I stood outside
in the glittering yard it was dawn.
A week? More, since you died?

Nobody said. It was just *Come here,
sahib, come quick*, and footfalls
splashing ahead to the compound gates.
There. They waved one arm, its arc

including all I could see: *Ganga*.
I thought of your narrow grave
underwater, and with it the fields
and feathery tracks where cattle

were drifting twice their size, and trees
sprouted astonishing packages: carpets
rolled and tied above water, a roost
for files of sodden, precarious birds.

*

Now sit, sahib. Sit here.
It was the holy man,
patting the veranda floor.
Good. His face caked white

and well-fed body
draped in a leopard skin –
a circus strongman
reading my life. *Sahib*.

You are a learned man.
Don't be afraid.
I am learned too: Hazlitt.
The beautiful Lake Poets.

You are lonely.
Eyes closed, and the ropes
of greasy hair. One hand
pressing his wire cage

and its parrot – a brilliant
green hat-feather tail.
You are lonely now.
His mesmerised voice

pausing, collecting itself.
You must go.
Your work here – finished.
Your factory – finished,

his head tipped sideways
and then: *No more!*
almost a shout.
These are your own thoughts.

He was gone –
a faltering stooped prance
down to the yard, dragging
one leopard's foot in the dust.

Lying before me
were grains of wheat,
a twig like a rib,
a charred, thick chupatty.

*

My life out of my hands. By autumn
two, perhaps three carpets a week.
Never enough. When I drove out
the weavers' houses were shells –

everyone working all day in their fields,
shovelling grey Ganges silt into banks,
scraping and patting their ditches.
They will come back to us.

That was Pradeep, seeking me out
at Christmas, swirling his drink.
But when? They must care for their land . . .
then a shrug, and a blank stare

away to the compound walls,
the drugged eucalyptus trees.
We shall see. Yes, we shall see.
We spoke without thinking,

leaving the date of our sale
still vague as the evening darkened
and *Well*, said Pradeep, *Well —
time we should change*. For the party,

he meant: Mirzapur Christmas Dance
at the Club. By ten I was there,
hearing The Inkspots *Bless you
for being an angel. Bless you for making*

*a new world just when the old
world crumbled so help-less-ly*.
The record round and round
with its spiralling grief for that room,

those swathes of tinsel and ivy,
those yellowing billiard cloths, those walls
dotted with cotton-wool snow
like slush wherever the glue showed through.

*

I woke at five to a bare house,
luggage already half way home.
My last morning: a delicate stripe
of sky strengthening under my door,

the chowkidar's shuffling steps
backwards and forwards, his cough,
and the phlegm with its soft scatter.
When I looked out he was gone —

his charpoy tipped to the wall,
and a torn-off toothbrush stick
thrown on the balcony steps.
Sahib. A voice loud in the hall.

The driver's come.
I was bowed in the yard
as somebody draped a garland on:
roses and gainders – a necklace

of tickling loops. *Goodbye, sahib.*
Goodbye, sahib. Goodbye.
I salaamed to the puckered faces
not daring to speak, and was blind

through the compound gates
and on for a mile of the swirling lane
until I leant forward.
Stop. Wait for me here

and knelt at your grave. This is
my tentative hand on your stone,
touching as if it were braille:
Beloved wife – their child. And this

is my hand at the window again,
clenching, unclenching, then smearing
a hole in its silvery glass. Listen;
footsteps have started already –

your father's, crossing the landing.
He calls to me: *Seven o'clock*,
and the bathroom door squeaks.
A lit-up milkfloat is whining

house by house down the street
and daylight begins. Sun is no more
than a white, widening slit. The sea
a blank horizon returning to grey.

Dangerous Play

Frances. You were the favoured son
they never had – a tomboy, Frankie-boy,
collar and tie through the garden gate
each early morning. *Not too far, though –*

be careful! Your father's voice was the ghost
of the terrace roses, his uniform smudged
behind slithering leaves. *I promise!*
Only as far as the road! If he could hear

he would think you meant Cairo Road,
and hopscotch in sight of the settlers' houses.
At eight, when his sluggish official car
ferried him down to Government House,

any old chalky grid was a sign of you –
your fist-clenched, stammering dance
flicking and juddering round in his head
like a handkerchief waving him off.

Or so you imagine. Or so you say,
when you're telling me late in bed,
and sleepy enough to confuse what was
with what you're beginning to dream.

All Africa knew how the settlers behaved.
Why should he think I was safe with them?
'Cut them in half, you'll find mostly gin'
– I can hear him now – 'They're out and outers'.

And what did they find when the Earl was killed,
I wonder? What kind of blood did he bleed?
You were going to smile, but a sigh
catches you out, and as quickly as that

you're asleep, swivelling round in my arms
so it seems you are trying to work yourself free.
I click off the light, and at once, with my eyes tight shut,
I can see you again, but this time close at my side

when we stop on a stretch of moonlit road
and discover the Earl, whoever he was, with his head
crammed through his knees on the floor of a car,
his evening dress speckled with glass. Listen:

that's the Savoy Orpheans, foxtrotting out
from a wireless slewed on his passenger seat,
and the car itself is climbing a rock
like a toy someone pretended could dance.

It might be an accident, that's what I say,
he was drunk – but no, an accident wouldn't explain
this gooey hole in the core of his ear
where you show me a bullet went in.

Not that you're with me for long. When you say
I'll go for some help; stay put, you've already gone,
your tie like a tongue flipped over your shoulder,
leaving me wandering round and round

[49]

on worn-out grass by the car. I am guessing
There must be some evidence here. Some footprints?
A cartridge case? But each step I take
explodes and disperses a ripple of dust

until I can scarcely be sure which footprints
are innocent: which ones are mine,
which yours, and which, supposing any are his,
belong to the killer – and whether or not

I should pay any heed to this whisper
which says out of nowhere *Don't look in the car;*
don't look at the Earl. It's as if I might find
that he has been changed into someone I know,

or into myself, and cannot be altered back
to a stranger again, not even by half sitting up
in the darkness beside you like this, reminding myself
I am home, completely awake, and seeing you still

with your beautiful boyish face on the pillow
almost concealed by your hair,
but clearly smiling at something
you will not remember tomorrow, which I cannot share.

The Dancing Hippo

In my country we are not good to animals.
A dog is a dog, however it might sit up
and beg, or run through fire; and a bear
riding a bicycle still wants to eat you.
I think you can see from my lack of illusion
I have some experience – so when I tell you
this story caused me distress, do not ignore me.

It's difficult, teaching a hippo to dance.
It takes for ever. They don't grow on trees,
and buying one meant that our modest circus
made do with a mothy lion for an extra year
and sold two singing seals. Then when she arrived,
our hippo, she ate like a creature possessed.
And the shitting! Continual diarrhoea, with her tail
dithering frantically, spraying it everywhere.
I have to admit, I wanted her sold at once,
or turned into curio waste-paper baskets.

But Nikoli reckoned she'd learn. Day after day,
and sometimes night after night, we'd hear
the Dance of the Sugar Plum Fairy (with whip
obbligato) twittering out of his tent, and *Move!*
Move! while he hopped around on the straw
as if it were burning his feet. A hippo able to judge
would have certainly thought he was mad; so it may,
I suppose, have been pity that led her to copy him –
learning a ponderous sideways prance, a shuffling reverse,
and a massive triumphant collapse (her curtsey).

That's what it looked like, at least,
the first time she danced for the public –
on a summer night in some one-horse place
we found by chance in the foothills,
with warm, mosquito-y, hop-smelling air blowing in
under the rolled-up flaps, and the people
transfixed by the prance, reverse,
and collapse that we thought was nothing,
but seemed to them like a miracle.

Maybe it was. For sure everyone loved her,
even when summer was over, and we returned
to perform in our permanent home, in the capital,
where they are used to marvels. On opening night
under the stars in the park, she excelled herself
in front of the President, rising at one time
(I think) on her chubby back legs for a second.
Afterwards Nikoli said she was not for this world
for long, and although he was right, his philosophy
wasn't enough to prevent the fire that burst
through her pen one night in the early new year
and burnt her to death, from breaking his heart.

We live in a country where animals count for little,
as I have said. But I remember him stumbling into my van
after the flames were doused, and the huge carcass
had gone wherever it went, gripping my arm,
leaning close to my face in the yellow glare
of my rickety kerosene lamp, and saying
I know it was useless, of course, her dancing.
I know. But God above it was beautiful!
Beautiful! God! – or something like that.

III

A Blow to the Head

On the metro,
two stops in from Charles de Gaulle,
somebody slapped my wife.

Just like that —
a gang of kids —
for moving her bag
from the seat to her lap:
a thunderclap
behind my back.

Very next thing
was reeling dark
and the kids outside
beside themselves:
You didn't see! You didn't see!
It might be him! It wasn't me!

For the rest,
she wept through every station into Paris,
her head on my shoulder like love at the start of its life.

*

By the merest chance
I had in mind
J. K. Stephen,
who damaged his head
on a visit to Felix-
stowe (Suffolk) in '86.

The nature of the accident is not certainly known;
in the Stephen family it was said he was struck
by some projection from a moving train.

Not a serious blow,
but it drove him mad
(molesting bread
with the point of a sword;
seized with genius—
painting all night),

and finally killed him
as well as his father,
who two years later
surrendered his heart
with a definite crack
like a sla...

    *

...which reminds me.
When I was a kid
a man called Morris
slapped my face
so crazily hard
it opened a room
inside my head
where plates of light
skittered and slid
and wouldn't quite
fit, as they were
meant to, together.

It felt like the way,
when you stand between mirrors,
the slab of your face
shoots backwards and forwards
for ever and ever
with tiny delays,
so if you could only
keep everything still
and look to the end
of the sad succession,
time would run out
and you'd see yourself dead.

*

There is an attic flat
with views of lead
where moonlight rubs
its greasy cream,

and a serious bed
where my darling wife
lies down at last
and curls asleep.

I fit myself
along her spine
but dare not touch
her breaking skull,

and find my mother
returns to me
as if she was climbing
out of a well:

ginger with bruises,
hair shaved off,
her spongy crown
is ripe with blood.

I cover my face
and remember a dog
in a reeking yard
when the kid I was

came up to talk.
I was holding a choc
in a folded fist,
but the dog couldn't tell

and twitched away –
its snivelling whine
like human fear,
its threadbare head

too crankily sunk
to meet my eye
or see what I meant
by my opening hand.

Look

I pull back the curtain
and what do I see
but my wife on a sheet
and the screen beside her
showing our twins
out of their capsule
in mooning blue,
their dawdlers' legs
kicking through silence
enormously slowly,
while blotches beneath them
revolve like the earth
which will bring them to grief
or into their own.

I pull back the curtain
and what do I see
but my mother asleep,
or at least not awake,
and the sheet folded down
to show me her throat
with its wrinkled hole
and the tube inside
which leads to oxygen
stashed round her bed,
as though any day now
she might lift into space
and never return
to breathe our air.

I pull back the curtain
and what do I see
but the stars in the sky,
and their jittery light
stabbing through heaven
jabs me awake
from my dream that time
will last long enough
to let me die happy,
not yearning for more
like a man lost in space
might howl for the earth,
or a dog for the moon
with no reason at all.

One Who Disappeared

Did you ever hear me tell
of that woman whose only son
was walking the cliffs at Filey
a month after moving up here

(imagine them as strangers
new from the fug of the west,
and keen to snuff up air
blasting straight out of Russia)?

If you did, then you'll have heard
how he footed the tufty edge
like a drunk walking a line,
pompously,

proud to think himself sober,
and how the smothering thump
of waves bursting in caves
drowned his giggly shout

when he floated up in a paw
of wind ripping over the cliff
like stubble-fire through a hedge
and immediately dropped away

as if he was young Mr Punch
whipped from a bare stage
and falling a hundred feet
on sheets of black rock.

Our boy is ill.
When I loom above
his panting hush
he scalds my face.

I look and look
and he's always there
on his soaked pallet.
I look once more

and see the woman
who watches her son
for the millionth time
in his final second

snatching a handful
of silver grass
from the chalk fringe
then leaving her

gaping,
clenching his fists
in the salt air
as hard on nothing

as I grip your hand
when you tiptoe in
and side by side
we gaze down

at our boy in silence,
like nervous spies
in an enemy country,
marooned on a beach

waiting for rescue,
scanning the sea
for a wink of light
which is hours overdue.

*

I'm awake to a thrush
doodling with its voice,
to the scratchy fuss of sparrows,
to a blackbird chinking loose change,

and day swirls into the street
like milk billowed through tea –
a big light lightening nothing
as it colours the maps of mountains

which is you beside me, sleeping,
that muzzy gap (the door),
and through it the luminous stripes
of the cot, lurching and snuffling.

Why do I feel that I've died
and am lingering here to haunt you?
Why don't I say your name?
Why don't I touch you?

I don't even feel I'm alive
when I hear the padded thwack
of the boy kicking round in his cot –
a soft crash, like the noise

of a splintered spar of wood
which falls in the night for no reason
a long way away in a builder's yard,
then is utterly still on the moonlit cement.

The Prague Milkbottle

for Ivo Smoldas
Spring 1989

The astrological clock
produces its twelve apostles
every hour

in a brainless jerking parade
as windows wheeze open and shut,
Death twitches,

bells ping, and the cockerel crows
like a model train at a crossing
while I

get drunk in the sunlit square with Ivo
surrounded by skirts as if nothing is wrong
except:

my bathplug won't fit the hole,
my water is cold,
my phone-call to home never works,
the exchange rate is shit,

and the milk!

– the milk of kindness, our mother's milk,
comes in a thing of French design,
looks like a condom and leaks like a sieve
and keeps us screaming most of the time.

*

In your wildest dreams you might whistle
and two ravens would flit their dark forest
for a baroque room you know is the British Embassy
(it has a view of Prague unmatched by the Palace).

The ravens turn into girls and are painfully beautiful,
leaning with bare arms entwined,
black dresses crushed to the back of a yellow sofa
to take in a view of the city you never expected to see from
                                                    this angle:

miraculous spires; ecstatic saints shattered by God;
and cobbled streets where the girls will squirm in your palm
then fold into wings and fly off with a gasp –
the sound of you waking alone in your dark hotel.

                    *

It's not suppression,
it's humiliation.

The men they put in power
(they aren't stupid) – some of them
can hardly speak a sentence.

It's not suppression,
it's humiliation.

I have a headache. Nothing much,
but threatening to be worse – a tension
like the silence in a clock before it strikes.

It's not suppression,
it's humiliation.

My chemist writes prescriptions
but we have no drugs. I wish him ill.
None of this has much to do with girls.

It's not suppression,
it's humiliation.

*

I leave Ivo to himself
but two hours later
he's outside the airport
hoisting a bag
of toys for my children.

It's like seeing the ghost
of a friend whose death
made you say everything
there was to say.
Now there is nothing.

The milk of kindness
floods our eyes,
or perhaps it's grit
swirled on the tarmac
in tottering cones.

We nod goodbye
where Security starts
and men in gloves
count my balls,
then I slither away

down a dingy tunnel,
and turn again
to Ivo pinned
on a block of light
the size of a stamp,

his mechanical arm
glumly aloft,
his mouth ajar
to show he is screaming
if I could just hear.

Hull

This is the park where Larkin lived
– moss-haired statues and dusty grass –
and a year or so after he'd packed and gone
        you lived here too

in one of those gaunt Victorian flats
where heat flies up to the ceiling and clings
in the intricate mesh of its moulding, leaving you
        frozen

whatever the weather, although it was freezing
in fact the day that I tried to persuade you
our life could go on, and we grappled for nearly
        an hour

on your hideous sofa (its bristling cloth
like tonsured hair which cannot grow back),
gasping and gritting our teeth and finally just
        giving up

whereupon you plunged into your jersey again
and picked up a book, while I – pretending
nothing unusual had happened – went to the window
        and saw

a man in a belted mac returning from work
– a respectable man: brown glasses and trilby hat –
stop under one of the cavernous chestnuts,
        fling

his briefcase heavily into the branches,
crouch in a hail of conkers, chase them
hither and yon in the cobwebby shade,
      pocket them,

then disappear in the gloaming along with the others
you learn to expect in this fish-smelling pastoral:
home-going clerks, litter-bin-lunatics, drunks,
      and those

who stand at their darkening windows and think
if they hurry there's time to get dressed and go out
and begin the day over again – with a visit, perhaps,
      to the plant-house

which glistens below, full of strangers who flounder
aimlessly round and round in its tropical bubble,
nod to each other through floppy-tongued leaves,
      and once in a while

stop at the cage where a moth-eaten minah bird
squats on its metal bough and says nothing at all
except – if you scare him badly enough –
      his name.

Missing

Tamworth.

Red brick on red brick.

An ogling eye in a greenhouse.

Lilac smoking in parched gutters and crevices.

A missing girl's head on lamp-post after lamp-post.

*

We had taken my mother's car
and driven into the blue –
she was in hospital then
and didn't care.

*

Out of nowhere, nowhere else to go,
stuck in the dead afternoon, stewed,

the mushroom hush of the lounge bar oozing up
through bilious carpet into our bed,

while men in the country nearby poked long rods
in voluptuous hedgerows, streams, rush-clumps,

fidgeting over the cracked hillsides shouting
She's not here, flinching at shadows, cursing.

*

We'd zigzagged over the map
seeing cathedral cities—
any excuse had done
to get us a week alone.

That evening under Southwell's
swarthy prolific leaves
an imp in a fissure of oak
might have been Robin Hood.

*

It was not for us. It was death—
though the men came back empty-handed,
and stacked their long poles in the yard.

They understood when we packed and paid.
There were other towns, sure – plenty,
if we could hurry – our last hour of day

squeezed by a storm fuming from Nottingham way:
pitch, lemon-yellow, beech-green,
champing till ready, flighting a few big blobs

as the dusty country we entered
braced itself – leaf-hands grasping,
toads under stones, mercury ponds blinking.

*

We'd kitted out the car
with a mattress in the back
and a sort of gyppo curtain
exactly for nights like this.

Before we left the suburbs
we posted my mother a card,
knowing my father would read it
stooping above her bed:

Fantastic carving at Southwell!
The car's going a bomb!
Not one puncture yet!
The back's really comfy!

*

The thing we did – the thing anyone like us did –
was find ourselves lost and be glad of it,
chittering to and fro in a lane-labyrinth
with its centre a stubble bank at the head of a valley.

Therefore we went no further. Therefore we simply sat
and watched the sky perform: elephant clouds at first
with their distant wobble and bulge like ink underwater,
then splits of thunder, then sour flashes of light

glancing off metal, then clouds with their hair slicked back,
edgy, crouching to spring, and when sprinting at last
fanned flat, guttering, flicking out ochre tongues
before losing their heads altogether, boiled down

to a skirt cartwheeling through woods,
a heavy boot squelching out squall after squall
of leaf-mould, nail, hair, and Christ knows what
shrieks and implorings we never caught even a word of.

*

We burrowed against each other
after the storm had gone,
and saw between our curtains
lightning over the valley

on its nimble silver legs –
one minute round our car,
the next high up in heaven,
kicking the splinters off stars –

then skipping away to somewhere
with the thunder-dog behind it
grumbling but exhausted,
and leaving us such silence

I'd swear I heard the moon
creak as it climbed the sky,
and the stubble field around us
breathing earth-smell through its bristles.

It is an Offence

The man in the flats opposite keeps a whippet
(once a racer) and two or three times a week
it craps by my front door – sloped, weary turds
like a single file of slugs in battle fatigues
(surprisingly slow for a whippet) – so that often
my shoes, my wife's, our children's bring it back home
to the stairs, the skirting, the carpets, the kitchen tiles
in bobbles or flakes or hanks or outrageous slithery smears.

The sad old dog doesn't know what he's doing, and yet
I'd still like to cover his arsehole with quick-set cement.

I admit that I also yearn to leave my mark on society,
and not see machines or people trample it foolishly.

On the one hand it's only shit; on the other, shit's shit,
and what we desire in the world is less, not more, of it.

IV

Lines of Desire

I A DREAM OF PEACE

It starts like this
with stick or stone
or sharpened bone

and a hill in the wilds
where a crotchety oak
soughs over a cave

and the face of fire
flares all day
all night all day

and *clink clinkety clink*
might be the hammer
of something new

or might be a bird
buried deep in the oak
which sings its heart out

with nothing to say
except what happens
to strike home next.

*

It starts like that and it comes to this:
my father's tank – *clank clankety clank* –

just one of hundreds, sprigged with leaves,
on a rippling road through northern France,

and blossoming light on apple trees,
and singing larks like dots in the sun,
and easy climbs and the summer wind,
and the...

*

In a twinkling the sun has vanished behind a barn, then it is
out again. A moment ago he would have sworn everything
looked like home – like Essex! But when he turns off the road
into a field it is not like Essex at all. On the bank of a stream is
a soldier's fair-haired head with no jaw to it, no mouth. This
is all he can find.

*

I wanted a big language for the people who died –
I wanted a big language for fighting. I found one,
but only when peace descended; then I looked back
and the apple-roads, my vanished brothers-in-arms,
the ruined flickering outskirts of the capital,
a dead dog in a pram, the enormous iron station
with its roof blown off, the herded people
all were part of my big language.
                                   I filled my lungs
and shouted until I had ripped the leaves from every tree in
                                                              sight
and raised a creamy wave on even the smallest buried lakes.
My language had conquered the world.
I was free to say what I wanted.

*

When I was a boy at the head of the stairs
my life was the life of the senses.
I cooled my face at a window above the yard

and saw in the melting distance a second boy
who could have been just like me but was not,
flapping his arms like someone about to take off

if only he could get free of the tangling grass
and the dull weight of his shoes, and the geese
he was driving ahead in a brilliant scattering cloud.

The grass, the wet, the melting light, the geese.
It was panicky, but it had something to do with peace.

        *

What should I die for?
Answer me that.
What should I live for?
Clickety clack.

Give me your answer.
Clickety clack.
Show me a war
then take it back.

        *

I fell in love with a soldier
seventy years younger than me,
who knew the country best
as soon as he left it to die.

Under a beech tree in Essex
he practised how it would go,
squeezing a gun barrel into his mouth
then deciding no.

But I knew nothing of that:
I only saw a soldier
hearing how death would be
in the dry crack of branches

echoing endlessly.

*

I knew nothing, or less than nothing.
I knew books.
I knew
'Gas! Gas! Quick, boys!'
and learnt it,
saying it slowly:
'Gas! Gas! Quick, boys!'
The wrong war, the wrong speed, the wrong accent.

Nobody noticed.
In the dusty classroom
sunlight went solid with dust.
Quick! Quick!
Slow. Slow.
My tongue turned heavily over
and sank in the deepest sleep.
I knew nothing, or less than nothing.
The wrong war, the wrong speed, the wrong accent.

*

Yes, I fell in love with a soldier
seventy years younger than me,
and after I had him by heart
I went to discover his grave.
This was not being brave.

Like mirrors, like snow, like chips of ice
white stones appear outside a wood.
Quick! Quick! It will soon be dark
and I won't be able to read their names
or come here again.

His voice ran by like a wave on a buried lake,
so quiet I had to hold my breath.
There it was then! A whisper and gone —
a secret I wanted to have as my own
if I ever got home.

*

I dreamed a woman made me take off my ring
(my father's ring) and at once I imagined a man
who stopped by a river somewhere up north from here
and threw in a ribbon which showed how brave he was.

Then in my dream the man was smothered by smoke
and I was aloft, catching the woman (the same woman)
up in my arms so we flew like a wounded gull,
me in my black, her in a rippling wedding-dress.

The whole country spread itself open below —
towns and villages, motorways, ring-roads, lanes,
water-logged moorland, grazing, a plain of wheat —
and we knew it contained whatever we meant by home.

The moon came out, and down we dipped close to the earth
where elm-tops tickled the woman's defenceless feet
and we searched for the intimate, beautiful detail in things:
a marbled starling, for instance, asleep on a telephone line.

By now I was tired and knew we had left it too late;
all we could see was wire, and too many eyes,
and a big gate like a grill wherever we went,
and a searchlight we could not escape for a moment longer.

We circled and circled, helplessly caught in each other,
not like a man and a woman at all, and not like a gull,
but a frivolous smidgin of paper blown up in a fire,
which twiddles away from the earth and cannot return.

*

What language to speak
in a world apart?
How to describe
peace in a heart?

My tongue woke up
but could not speak.
I opened my mouth:
clink clinkety clink.

*

They kept on jumping up, their happiness like a trampoline,
and set to at once. Chunks came away, rare as moonrock, or
fragments spiky with thick brown wire, or a whole door-
shaped section blurted over with writing. You couldn't read
what it said, no sentence came away complete, so what they
carried off were gasps and grunts.

We slumped in our armchairs watching, my father and I, and I wanted to know: did he recognise any of this? He shook his head while I imagined the ruined flickering outskirts, the enormous iron station with its roof blown off.

'It must make you wonder?'

'Yup' was all he would say, 'Yup,' and kept on looking away.

*

Change the channel.

With our son between us
asleep and dreaming
the news floats up
in a blaring wash.

Press the button.

Now here is a soldier
who stands in the desert
and shouts a language
I do not know.

Change the channel.

Oh, but I see:
it's 'Gas! Gas! Gas!'
rattled so fast
it means nothing to me.

Press the button.

Now here is a tank
overtaken by camels –
it makes no sense.
Clank clankety clank.

Change the channel.

Oh, but I see:
the camels are leaving
the world where no one
expects to survive.

Press the button.

Now here is the nothing
we see in the dark
when pictures stop
and voices die.

Change the channel.

Oh, but I see:
it's not nothing at all –
two faces are there
in the creaking drizzle,

faint and silent,
while rising between them
the child wakes up
and cries to be fed.

Press the button.

*

There's nothing special in this goodbye at my father's house:
too much to drink, too much to eat, too many rooms too
                                        warm,

and the talk slowing down to traffic and the best and worst
                                        way home
in a language not exactly dead but not exactly living.

So let the music start. Then comes the spurt of tyres on gravel.
My father turns back to his house like someone walking
                                        underwater.

2 MONEY SINGING

It starts with the scream
of a porcupine saw
in a forester's yard.

It ends with the clunk
of walnut doors
in velvet halls.

It starts with the flash
of a furnace fire
under melting sand.

It ends with the chink
of crystal glasses
at priceless parties.

It starts with the clack
of a blurred shuttle
in furry air.

It ends with the sssh
of a satin slip
on a shaved leg.

*

There is mist rolling over the ground which is not mist and
not fog either, denser than both of them and darker, but when
it wraps itself round trees like mist or fog the birds stop
singing just as they do in mist or fog – a few forlorn cheeps
then silence and a lack of direction, the sense of happiness
snuffed out for ever.

No, it is not like mist or fog at all. It is a yellow gas-cloud
and the trees have no birds and no leaves or buds either, they
are skeletons, skeletons wringing their hands at the grotesque
moon-mess of mud they stand up in, and over which now,
wearing pig-masks and ant-eater noses, unexpectedly stumble
a line of soldiers. They would be shouting if there were
anyone alive to hear them shout; as it is they hiss, floundering
under the bare trees, working forward to where the air seems
brightest, the yellow mist or fog rolls away, then throwing
down their heavy rucksacks and weapons like men who no
longer care to know about defeat or victory or anything else,
tearing off their noses and pig-masks so we can see their very
own eyes are the wide bulging enormous things we thought
must have been glass, and charging down on us each with one
hand thrust forward to show the small coin we gave them
before any of this started.

*

Now here's a march that everyone knows
– *diddle de dumpty, dozhi doh* –
strap on your rucksack and tie up your shoes.

We're walking the country from north to south
–*diddle de dumpty, dozhi doh*–
so people can see what we say is the truth.

Cameras pop and our faces go
–*diddle de dumpty, dozhi doh*–
like leaves stripped from a sapling bough.

They fly in the air, they're no longer ours
–*diddle de dumpty, dozhi doh*–
and settle in crackling newspapers.

Now here they are on the classroom wall
–*diddle de dumpty, dozhi doh*–
a story which might not have happened at all.

*

I think I am about to lift my head,
my young head on young shoulders,
in the first classroom of my life.

I think I am about to step into these pictures,
alongside these marchers and goggle-eyed soldiers.
I think I am going to find out about money.

But the story breaks and I am left out.
Other soldiers appear, this time jammed in a boat
more like a tin trunk than a boat, which stops

on a white beach in France where the soldiers
spill out as if they were shy children arriving at a party.
This one, here, cannot stand it so sits down and cries:
he wants his mother. This one here is my father

[89]

and wants to change his trousers, to start off dry.
He wants to be neat and tidy if he is going to die.

He is thinking that if he lifts his head,
his young head on young shoulders,
he might see what something in this is worth.

He is thinking that somewhere over the sand dunes
in the solid world of roads and towns with civilians
he might discover someone to give him back what he has lost

if he can work out what that might be, and how much it cost.

＊

Money is getting noisier.
He comes home at night
with figures jingling in his head.

Money is getting taller.
It whistles down at him
from new scaffolding in the old sites.

Money is getting long-faced.
It keeps his fingers busy
when he would rather be undoing a button.

Money is getting ambitious.
It wants him to sell his old banger
and sit a girl down beside him in comfort.

＊

My mother and father
were Adam and Eve

back to the garden
hand in hand,
forgiven and blameless,
their lives their own.

But this was no garden:
this attic flat
was an eye on the Thames
blinded with rain,
their landlord's dog
a wolf at the door.

They didn't care;
for all they knew
love was the roof
above their heads,
love paid bills
and kept them fed.

By night they took
their deckled ledger
and counted the cost
of the life to come:
a child's clothes; a cot.

By day they wiped
their windows and saw
heavyweight, slow
dredgers explore
rich shipping-lanes below.

*

What does money feel like?
Tell me, tell me true:
Squelchy, greasy, slippy, wet;
that's what I tell you.

What does money feel like?
Tell me, since you know:
Burning, panting, rasping, dry;
that's what I tell you.

*

Softened-up, scrubbed, somewhere
between waking and sleeping
in the night-light dark
I become myself for the first time
when the bedroom door opens
and this ogre my father appears,
silent and drooping-shouldered
against the harsh passage light.

His one eye is a cigarette
reddening furiously as he steps
right up to me, bends close,
and leaks smoke into my hair;
there is a quick stir of bristles,
a saliva-smack, a half-grunt,
and I lie completely still
pressing one hand to my cheek,

about to wipe his kiss off
or rub it in, I cannot decide,
and think that beyond his smoke
I catch the unhappy smell of work,
in the way I might see a fish
flick through a brown stream
which on first looking in I thought
was water, and water only.

*

I take a leaf out of a book
  I listen to money singing

I find an attic to call my own
  I think about soldiers counting

I look through a ceiling-window
  I hear a rifle firing

I lie in an empty bed
  I dream of a heart beating

I turn my eyes inward
  I catch a woman flying

I see...

*

I saw money in the distance
like an enormous wave,
its ragged lip
churning up bits of engine

bobbins, empty paint-pots,
chimneys, and toppling forward
with the packed roar of voices
together but incomprehensible,

though as they came closer
lessening, an ordinary shout
rushing into trenches,
oozing along gun-barrels,

flash-flooding the bomb-sites
in city-centres, drowning rubble,
and all the time quieter,
gradually shrivelling

until not like a wave at all
but a strong and steady tide
dimpling across grazing,
swilling round new factories,

rising through wires and cables,
and filling computer screens
flashing their busy green numbers
in perfect silence. Perfect silence.

*

The roof over our heads
weighs so disastrously much
when it falls it will crush us all in our beds.

The world wants me to know
our children could reach up
and stave off this weight from us sheltering below.

Our children are asleep;
they have no idea
how fast this weight might drive us into the earth or how
                                                    deep.

Our lives are our own.
Fall, roof, fall,
if that's what it takes to show me where I am most at home.

  *

Last thing, I take out the empties.
There's frost on the doorstep,
frost on the paving-stones,
a skin of frost on the ash-buds
over-reaching the garden wall.

I'm tired, but just for now
I can feel the world is mine
for as little or much as I want;
I can lean against my house
and not even feel the cold.

Due south at the end of the street
the City of London's towers
are blinking their million eyes:
I can meet their level gaze
and pretend they are nothing to me.

My empties make their mark:
a brittle, nipped-off crash.
And still there's no one about.
Not a siren-song. Not a dog.
No breeze through the iron ash.

When I was a boy with my father right behind me
he shooed me out one day in the early morning
with a gun tucked under my arm and said: Why not
walk round for an hour and see what you can find?

I followed our tatty hedge which led me past
the Ashground, then the pond filled in with bricks,
then the Council tip, and then the water-meadows
where I stopped, felt the emptiness, and wanted to go back.

I saw the hoar-frost sunlit on a line of sycamores
which staggered with the river in its twisting bed;
I heard the snow-crust hardening the grass which creaked
and grumbled as I flicked the safety-catch and moved ahead.

I hated it: the signs of people, then the lack of them;
the ugliness, and then that crystal beauty flooding in.
I don't know why. My feelings were my own.
My life was mine. My life was everything.

So when the hare appeared I didn't hesitate.
Before it cleared the line of sycamores I had it
covered, waiting for my moment, which was when
it sat down door-stop still, the long ears brindled white,

the short-lashed eyes, the split and quizzical top lip all fixed
for ever as I bowled it over, so at any time thereafter
I might call them up, and see the blood-filled nose again,
the clotted fur, the gleaming brain wide open to the air

as I do now, tip-toeing forward through the bedroom dark
towards you in your cot to hear you breathe, to loom above
your milky-smelling body and your hare-lipped face
for no especial reason, just for love.

4   LINES OF DESIRE

It starts with a father
who climbs his son
and weighs him down
begging to live:
it starts with love.

It starts with a roof
of paper money
the slightest breeze
might blow into space:
it starts with love.

It starts with a child
whose stitched-up face
is a whiskery cat
learning to smile:
it starts with love.

It starts with the word
you breathe in my ear
which enters my heart
with a thundering roar:
it starts with love.

*

This soldier I loved, the soldier seventy years younger than me: when he died his widow wanted a silence where she might see him again. She sent the children to her sister, drew the curtains, lay in her bed, and ordered straw to be spread on the cobbles outside, so that when wheels passed by, or horses, they would be no more than a whisper.

This lasted for years. Then the children came home, the curtains opened, the stamped-down straw blew away, and she had her life back, only it was never exactly her life again. She heard of a man who had known her soldier, and discovered him miles away in a locked room with one ceiling-window, nothing to read or listen to, and nothing he could break – nothing like a vase or a cup – because what could be broken might also be a weapon.

When she saw him a second time she took a map with her, to show off the country her soldier had known by heart. Now they sat on the bed in silence, ambling through springing woods, sliding down chalk banks, dabbling the brown water in gravel pits, and at the end of everything walking off side by side along a wide cart-track, each in their own dry runnel of mud, a low grass wall between them but nevertheless like lovers, letting the track take them wherever it wanted, leaving no footprints.

*

They are my mother and father,
this couple walking before me,
each in the rut of a cart-track
somewhere deep in the country.

My father is home on leave
with pollen-dust on his toe-caps;
my mother's legs are bare
and flecked with bright straw-scratches.

It's years before I am born
and they've still to imagine me;
I'm merely the ghost in the hedgerow
which might be the wind or a bird.

I'm bound to stay behind them
all day while the cart-track dawdles
here and there past chalk-pits
and sullen, green-eyed ponds.

I only leave when I've seen her
working her hand through his arm,
when I've heard him speak her name
in a whisper like never before.

*

Right at the back
half-listening
half-dreaming
I open my eyes
in the dusty classroom
to learn about love
and Marcus Brutus
an honourable man
clanks off the page
his judicious tongue
swelling out of his mouth
to roll the earth

in a new direction
and raise a wave
on its buried lakes.

Then I shut my eyes
on the swirling dark
of lunatic atoms
and Portia appears
in a moonlit garden
of holly and ice
which is bitter to see
but never so painful
as she is herself
who has swallowed fire
which fills her mouth
and her long throat
then drops clean through
to her sizzling heart
and won't go out.

Then I open my eyes
on Brutus once more
and discover by now
he has learnt about love
and thrown himself down
on his stupid sword
while the air rocks
in my dusty classroom
and silence falls
so deep I can hear
the earth return
on its creaking axle
to just where it was

and a wave die down
on its buried lakes.

*

Dum dum de dum, de dum de dum de start
clack clackety clack, clack clackety clack clack see
diddle di da da, diddle di da da heart.

Clack clackety clack, clack clackety clack clack burn
diddle di da da, diddle di da da me
dum dum de dum, de dum de dum de learn.

Diddle di da da, diddle di da da give
dum dum de dum, de dum de dum de free
clack clackety clack, clack clackety clack clack live.

*

Then I met you and was lifted up from the world
once more, up from our bed, up through the roof
and into the air, the air which touched us lightly
as cloth, yet also seemed solid and heavy as water.

We circled a while, inspecting the streets we knew —
the pavements crazed with familiar cracks, the square
which is really a circle, the plane trees
raising their dusty hands to snatch at our feet —

but we were free, and spreading our wings
swooped off to a different part of the city
where sirens wept, and crowds of querulous faces
loomed like coins in a fountain, except they were shouting,

until we flew on, and reached that zigzag line
which marks the edge of the town, the scrap yards
and unfinished houses where street lamps take long strides
then end, and the moon comes out at last

soaking the huddles of woodland, the hedges
sprinting for cover, the white-washed gabled farms—
and stopped, both of us treading the air
and staring silently down at the country below,

finding the easily overlooked tracks,
the secret runnels, the pathways buried in grass,
the short cuts and fenced-off lanes, the lines of desire,
the furtive steps up hillsides or deep under trees—

as if every footprint that we had set down on the world
were still to be seen, and we could be sure
which trails we had followed were false, which true,
and where we were lost before we came into our own.

*

starling-song

from the telephone wire
plugged into my house

down

scratchy-dry this late dusk
but sweet still while I wait

here

on my worn doorstep to catch you
last thing over the threshold

now

body and fixing listening head
like a tuning fork tingling

soon

the note bubbling
then steady in my own throat

*

Home –
shaking office-smoke from your hair,
the unhappy money-taste on your skin:
wherever you are, I will be there too.

Kitchen –
eyes closing and mouth sunk into a pout,
tongue stumbling between food and talk:
wherever you are, I will be there too.

Bedroom –
winded silk shirt collapsing on to a chair,
tights too spindly and thin to make it:
wherever you are, I will be there too.

Bedside –
picking across the miles of difficult carpet,
air-current holding you up but only just:
wherever you are, I will be there too.

Bed –
beautiful heavy marionette with your strings cut,
then tightening as you roll over to face me:
wherever you are, I will be there too.

*

In their universe above my head
our children are gunning each other down,
hunting the enemy from doorway to doorway,
braining a doll on the stairs, up-ending a box
of rocket launchers and tanks: *clank clankety clank*.

I am at work in my room underground,
my pen itching a sheet of paper,
dreaming up ways to stop the roof falling,
then pushing my chair back and staring
at nothing on earth: *dum dum de dum*.

Into my head flows a crooked stream
with sycamores flourishing round it,
a flat meadow of frozen grass,
and a hare which staggers when my shot hits
but darts off perfect and unbloodied: *hey nonny*.

*

I came to the edge of the world –
where the crumbling sky
rests on the roof-tops all day drizzling lead,
where the acid sea
has bleached the pink from gulls' feet,
where the exhausted smoking earth
grows nothing.

It happened today.

I wanted to give you my love but when I tried I couldn't get
through,
so I left my hotel and walked along the coast road into the
city:
the rain fell hard, stinging my face,
and steamed-up taxis slowed as they drew level then sped off
honking.

I found an empty bar and another telephone
but the lines were still down, and when I craned into the
darkness
I could hear the miles crackle, could see the wind and sleet
filling the spaces between us.

You were nowhere,
and when I shut my eyes tight
I felt rooted into that sour ground.
I could even sense the earth
turning,
the fire at its heart nearly out,
the cold
seeping through galleries of black stone
into the soles of my shoes.

I gave up
and walked back into the rain.
You were somewhere,
I knew that, at least, not here but somewhere,
and I would find you
as long as I went on looking.

I came to the market square in the old town
and my feet rang on the huge glistening cobbles
while beneath me soldiers still fought hand to hand
along sewers and stinking barrel-vaulted drains.

Above my head the chipped bell in the bell-tower
still sent its flat message into the countryside
and a man crossing his farmyard suddenly hesitated,
looked up, then hurried indoors for his rifle.

In front of me the pastel-coloured houses rose:
a ragged wave, still swirling the lives of their fathers,
mothers and children, their sheets, hearthstones, carpets,
everything down on me to sweep me away.

When I found a path through
I was on the old road again,
the one winding back to my hotel
along the dockyard wall,
bringing me out at last on the beach
so I knew where I was.

My shoes sank into the sand, and the rain redoubled its
                                        efforts,
yet when I reached the pier and saw the lights of my hotel
shining ahead of me weakly but plainly,
I nevertheless turned aside and walked out over the water,
to the slipped-tile hut where the wind was fiercer than ever,
the waves a darker brown and more turbulent, the cloud
                                        thicker,
and the few gargoyle-fishermen too sad to pay me any
                                        attention.

I did this purposefully,
as though I had a reason.

As though the fishermen might speak to me
in a language I could admire.

As though they might tell me it was true
the soldiers had laid down their weapons.

As though everything I knew to be complicated
was in fact easy.

As though the price of everything
had finally been agreed.

As though the past was really the past
and I had escaped it.

As though I could grip the rail with both hands,
lean over,
and see the waves change from brown to translucent blue,
the wind drop,
and you,
at liberty in the clear water of your own life,
with oxygen slithering from your mouth and nose
and water-ropes twisting from your fingers and toes,
rising steadily towards me through the reflection of my face.

V

Salt Water

The village of Orford, five miles south of Aldeburgh on the Suffolk coast, survived for centuries as a fishing port; now it is separated from the sea by the river Alde, and by a strip of land known as the Ness. The Ness is ten miles long, stretching from Slaughden to North Wear Point. It is overlooked by a twelfth-century castle, and is also known as the Spit and the Island.

During the First World War, the Armament Experiment Flight of the Central Flying School was stationed on the Ness, which became a site for parachute testing and, later, a firing and bombing range. In the late 1930s Orford Research Programme was founded, and the Ness became a Listening Post and a centre for experimental work on radar. It was later taken over by the Atomic Weapons Research Establishment, and laboratories were built in which the triggers for nuclear bombs were tested; these were closed down in 1971. The Ness was then cleared by the Explosive Ordnance Disposal Unit. It was sold to the National Trust in 1993.

In the reign of King Henry II, when the village still faced the sea, a local historian recorded the capture of the Orford Merman. This Merman was kept in the castle, where *whether he would or could not, he would not talk, although oft-times hung up by his feet and harshly tortured*. Eventually he was released into the harbour.

In the late eleven-fifties
when the river and the sea
were still in one another's arms
and lived in harmony

there came a summer day so hot
the sea seemed hardly wet,
and the fishermen remained at home
until the sun had set,

had set and rustled up a breeze
and high tide at the full,
so just like that their sails were out
beyond the harbour wall.

A mile offshore, before the shape
of home had slipped away,
they hushed, and cast their clever nets
like grain into the bay.

One hour passed. Another hour.
The house lights on the land
began to jitter and go out,
the darkness to expand,

and silence in a steady flood
rushed round them silkily,
and even filtered through their nets
to calm the rocking sea.

No iron-filing shoal of fish
criss-crossed the rock-strewn floor,
no oyster winked, no battling crab
stuck out an angry claw,

the clear-cut worlds which make the world
lost all their difference,
the sea was sky, deep down was high,
and nonsense seemed like sense.

Enough like sense, at least, to mean
that in the red-eyed dawn,
with courses set and sails poised
to catch the first wind home,

it seemed the sort of miracle
that no one thought was rare
for one of them to haul on board
his streaming net and there

to find a merman large as life –
a merman! – half death-pale,
half silver as a new-made coin
and fretted like chain-mail.

*

For a million years one life simply turns into the next –
the spider hangs between driftwood and sea holly,
the sparrow hawk balances exactly over a shrew,
the hare sits bolt upright and urgent, all ears:
there is no reason why any of this should change.

But a new thought arrives and the island is invaded –
a radio mast stands up and starts cleaning its whiskers,
a field of mirrors learns to see clear beyond the Alps,
a set of ordinary headphones discovers the gift of tongues:
there is no reason why any of this should change.

Work goes ahead smoothly but no one breathes a word –
a slim needle is sensibly embarrassed by the red,
a pressure gauge puffs out its cheeks but is always steady,
a bird-walk of mathematics knows just where it is going:
there is no reason why any of this should change.

*

Not rare? Not like a miracle?
No, not until he spoke,
when feebly as a rotten thread
the spell that held them broke

and every clear-cut bit of world
snapped back into its place:
the sea was sea, the sky was sky,
the merman's face his face,

which slid between its salty lips
an eel-dance of a tongue,
a tongue which could not fix or shape
the words it splashed among.

This made the fishermen afraid;
it told them they had caught
a devil deaf to every law
their own religion taught,

or else, perhaps, a different god
they could not understand
but had to honour and obey
when they returned to land.

*

To create an explosion is the point of all this,
an explosion neither too soon nor too late,
an explosion precisely where it needs to be,
over the head of an enemy.

Not yet.

Scientists arrive to test triggers for the explosion,
triggers which must boil like hell and also be frozen,
triggers which must shake themselves silly and still work,
still know how to create a vacuum.

Not yet.

Weird laboratories spring up for these triggers,
Chinese pagoda-roofs which will protect the triggers
and which in the case of an accident with the triggers
will collapse and bury everything.

Not yet.

But it turns out that the vacuum cannot wait to be born,
the vacuum feeds itself on the very idea of discovery,
the vacuum wants to swallow the whole village and show
the explosion might as well already be over.

Not yet.

*

They made their choice; they froze their hearts;
they bound the merman's wrists
and wound him tightly in their net
with clumsy turns and twists;

then swerved towards the shore again,
and just as sunlight came
above the crescent harbour wall
they brought their trophy home.

Wives and children crowded round,
mouths gaping with surprise,
and gaping back the merman cried
baleful, senseless cries,

cried tears as well as sighs and sobs,
cried gulps, cried gasps, cried blood,
cried out what sounded like his soul
but never cried a word.

This made the fishermen afraid
again, it made them guess
the merman might have come to them
to put them through a test

and they, by cruelly catching him,
marooning him in pain,
and putting him on show like this
had blundered into sin.

*

Then the triggers are ready, they neither boil
nor freeze, they spin at any speed you please,
and are carried off like gifts in velvet boxes.

Then the bomb disposal men pick to and fro
with their heads down, each one carefully alone
and quiet, like pioneers prospecting for gold.

Then the radio masts die, their keen whispers
and high songs go, their delicate necks bow,
and voices fill up the air without being heard.

Then the field of mirrors folds too, its flat glare
shatters and shuts up, cannot recall the highest Alp
or anything except types of cloud, come to that.

Then the waves work up a big rage against roof-tiles
and breeze blocks, against doors, ventilation shafts, clocks,
and moon-faced instrument panels no one needs any more.

Then the wind gets to work. It breaks into laboratories
and clapboard sheds, it rubs out everything everyone said,
clenching its fingers round door jambs and window frames.

Then the gulls come to visit, shuffling noisily
into any old scrap-metal mess, settling on this for a nest,
and pinning their bright eyes on bare sky overhead.

And in due season flocks of beautiful shy avocets—
they also come back, white wings scissored with black,
calling their wild call as though they felt human grief.

*

They wound a rope around his net
and dragged him through the square,
up the looming castle keep,
then down the castle stair

and down and down and down and down
through wet-root-smelling air
into a room more cave than room
and hung him there.

Not hung him up until he died,
but hung him by his tail,
his tail which shone like silver once
and crinkled like chain-mail,

then built a fire beneath his head
to see if he could learn
the language that he still refused,
plain words like *scare*, like *burn*,

and other words like *agony*,
like *hatred*, and like *death*,
though hour by hour not one of these
weighed down the merman's breath.

This made the fishermen afraid
once more; it made them see
that somehow they the torturers
had set their victim free.

*

The waves think their hardest task
is to work each stone into a perfect O;
the marram thinks all it must do
is hold tight and not trouble to grow.

There's no story, never a point of view,
there's nothing here that's trustworthy or true.

Each grain of salt thinks it is able to see
over the highest Alp with its pure white eye;
the sea holly thinks it alone
can support the whole weight of the sky.

There's no clue, never a word in your ear;
there's nothing here that's justified or clear.

Winter storms think they will bring
the worst news anyone can bear to be told;
the east wind thinks it can certainly blow
colder than the coldest possible cold.

There's no code, never an easy cure;
there's nothing here that's definite or sure.

*

They cut him down. They hauled him up
the whirlpool of the stair,
they dragged him past their wives and children
gawping in the square,

and silently, as though the words
they used to know before
were all dead now, they carried him
down to the shingle shore.

They slid him tail-first in the sea
and washed the bitter drops
of blood-crust from his finger ends
and salt-spit from his lips,

and all the while, still silently,
they watched the tide bring in
a brittle, dimpled, breaking flood
of silver through his skin,

then open up his glistening eyes
in which they saw their fear
rise up to greet them one last time
and fade, and disappear,

disappear while they stood back
like mourners round a grave,
and watched his life ebb out of theirs
wave by wave by wave.

Reading the Elephant
for Ted Hughes

I won't say much about it now, except that she got
bored, or I did, at any rate someone left someone,
there was a leaving, and quite by chance
I had this friend of a friend who said why not
run away for a bit, it won't seem like running,
it won't when you say it's to Africa, God no,
that sounds like choice. So I did. I went like a shot.

And the next thing I knew was this place
marooned in the trees – that is: in the hills,
except it was trees I could see, no two the same
and swarming right up to the house – one with a face
in its trunk like a skinny-jawed Rackham witch,
one a cedar of some sort though really like clouds,
slabs of green cloud which boiled straight up into space.

It had people there too, of course, but they left me
as well, or rather I chose to stay put. Come morning
they'd clatter out into the jeep with their hampers,
their cameras, their hip-flasks, and set off to see
whatever strayed into their paths (one day a lion
shagged out on a comfortable branch, the next a croc
rip-roaring a bambi, just like they do on TV).

I'd walk round in circles indoors and wait until no one
was looking – in circles, but never unhappy, just
turning time back on itself. You know how it is.
Then I'd slither away to a spot where the sun
splayed down through those trees I was talking about

like a bicycle wheel, and set myself square to the world
as though everything in it had only that moment begun.

I mean: as though never till then had the daylight
come razoring over that silver-grey scrub,
never till then had the dust of that infinite landscape
been glued into cones of such a miraculous height
by ants with such staggering brains, never till then
had leaves been shelter or simply the things that they were –
pure pattern, pure beauty, pure pleasure in living, pure sight.

They never last long, these moments. With half a chance
we drop back to life as it is. I understand that.
I'm not quite a fool. So to keep myself airborne I always
snapped open some book (some parachute) just as my trance
was ending – which meant on the day that I'm thinking about
I'd turned to Pierre and was hearing how Moscow must fall
this month, what with the winter, what with the French
                                        advance.

Soldiers fanned out on the steppes. Feathers of smoke
flapped above burnt-out farms. An immense chandelier
reflected bare shoulders and medals revolving in miniature,
time and again, as the string quartet for a joke
performed by a wide-open window for Boney to hear,
each note struck fierce and hard and long on the dark
like stones sent skittering out on a windless lake –

like something inside me, yet outside as well,
a fracture, a cracking, which made me whisk round,
heart jumping, and find there not ten yards behind,
stock still in the African day I could no longer tell
was real – an elephant. Elephant.

Huge as a hill, creased where the weather runs down,
grave-grey in the haze of its dry-grass-pissed-on smell

and staring me out. That lasted I don't know how long —
the eyes not blinking no matter how busily flies
kept fussing and dabbling, the ragged-edged ears
traced with lugubrious veins, the bristly thong
of its tail twitched side to side, and me just sitting
not thinking at all — at least, me thinking that never
would one of the several worlds I was living among

connect with another, that soon I would just disappear
as the elephant would, its baggy-skinned legs
slow-pumping, its tentative feet squashing down
on their silent compressors, and leaving the air
disturbed for only a moment, no more, as I did myself
when I saw that enough was enough, and escaped
from the trees into unbroken sunlight with everything clear.

The Spoilt Child

It was a privilege to ride out
from the stables with his mother:
the world belonged to them,
they belonged to each other,

and the labrador puppy slinking
beside them in and out of the hedge –
she belonged to them too;
she was part of the privilege,

trotting to heel just like that
as soon as the order came,
so all three seemed like mechanical toys
whose journey was always the same,

always began in the deep blackberry lane
softly, hooves cushioned on gravel,
then unwound gradually into the village
where mother and son appeared at window-level

trying hard not to stare in
through veils of variously figured lace
at lives they were happy to see lived
as long as each knew its place.

Here they never quite came to a halt,
only pretended they might be slowing
down sometimes for *Thank you; thank you –*
and now, really, we must be going,

before clopping on towards open country,
their minds filled with nothing—
or rather, filled with the thought
of lush meadows, hooves thundering,

and every horizon they might choose to face
splitting open like water in front of a prow,
or splitting like earth itself
under the keel of a plough,

and going on splitting until—
as if it were dust striking his eye—
the boy saw a dog, a bull terrier,
apparently drop from the sky

and flatten the beautiful labrador puppy
still trotting neatly at his side,
roll her so she was pale belly side up,
plant his bow legs astride,

and latch onto her neck. What comfort
then was his mother, shutting her eyes?
She might give her little scream,
she might cry,

but the outrageous teeth stayed locked
in the sleek golden throat,
and when the boy at last dismounted to look
they were bright shining wet

with the brilliant life-blood of his pet,
making him feel he was no use at all
no matter how he might thwack his whip
on the bull terrier's head, and call

for his beloved to rise up and fight,
and go on using his whip again, then again
and again, until at last giving way
when a stranger butted in –

a beery man wearing a vest,
and undone, down-trodden shoes,
who carried an all-metal hammer
and a stone he intended to drive through

the bull terrier's teeth to shatter them
if there was no chance of prising them loose,
which he decided at once there wasn't,
giving one, two, three steady blows,

with the pop-eyed boy watching
and the mother now covering her face,
before sinking down onto his knees:
Jesus; Jesus. Right then – in that case –

and finally hammering the stone
so far in, it stuck out the other side
of the terrier's foaming mouth,
opening it up wide

and leaving the puppy's neck plain
for the boy to see:
the pink windpipe, the oyster-coloured muscles
like a lesson in biology.

Sorry, I'm sorry, the mother and son
then thought they would hear the man say.
What they got was a single deep grunt
and a slow turn away—

It's all right, he said. *I'll deal with her now.*
It's all right. It's all right. Ah, but you see
they thought he was lying. Nothing was right
any more, nothing could change history—

and now, if nobody minded...?
They set off home at the trot, and never looked round
once at the stranger watching them go, his dog in pain,
their own splayed on the ground.

Dead March

It's twenty years (*It's not, it's twenty-three—*
be accurate) since you were whisked away
(*I wasn't 'whisked away': I broke my skull*)
and I was left to contemplate your life.
(*My life? Ridiculous. You mean my death.*)

Well, twenty/twenty-three. I can't decide
if that's a long time or no time at all,
or whether everything I've said since then,
and thought, and done, to try and work out how
the way we treat our lives might be involved
with how our lives treat us is more than just
a waste of breath. That's right. A waste of breath.

You see, you're always with me even though
you're nowhere, nothing, dead to all the world—
you interrupt me when I start to talk,
you are the shadow dragging at my heels.
This means I can't step far enough away
to get the thing I want you to explain
in focus, and I can't lean close enough
to hear the words you speak and feel their weight.

And if I could, what difference would it make?
It's like I said. I can't decide. It's just
that having you suspended all these years
at some clear mid-point between life and death
has made me think you might have felt your way

along the link between the two, and learnt
how one deserves the other. Or does not.

I feel I'm standing on a frozen pond
entranced by someone else below the ice,
a someone who has found out how to breathe
the water and endure the cold and dark.
I know I ought to turn my back. I can't.
I also know that if I just stay put
and watch the wax-white fingers flop about
I'll start to think they must be beckoning.
I stare and stare and stare and stare and stare.
It's twenty years since you were whisked away,
or twenty-three. That's more than half my life.

Does That Hurt?

With grass on the quarry floor knee-high;
with invisible larks showering down song
from the far side of the sky;

with oak-scrub and bramble the only shade;
with ants in their deep forest keeping track
of every journey they've made;

with glittering flint-hills gradually bleeding sand;
with the body of one rusting mechanical digger
stooped over its snapped-off hand;

with my small son steadily smaller at my side;
with what we have left of the quarry to cross
stretching too wide, too wide;

with a dog-rose barrier guarding the high ledge ahead;
with hearts hobbling when finally we flop there
shot-down-dead;

with a fat stinging bee dropping out of a flower well-fed;
with the same bee losing its grip on the air and stumbling
onto my son's head;

with screaming and panic which swipes the poison in;
with my pantomime brushing and flapping *keep still!*
achieving nothing;

with the entire horizon a tight circle of pain;
with the flint-hills, the long-drawn-out quarry floor
hateful to think of again;

with larks still rising out of the world in their crazy trance;
with the earth itself crying the cry
of mere existence.

*

It's not just him I see,
not just his soft weight
I lift and bring with me,

no, not just him, it's you,
your weight as well,
your pain brand-new

however long it lasts,
which now means years,
means each day still your first

at sea, unwillingly afloat,
your big high-pillowed bed
a raft which marks the site

where everything you knew
went down, and you the one
survivor spared to show

the way pain looks, and loss,
and life alone,
and grief without redress:

its sticky breath,
its tongue which cannot budge and longs
to ask for death.

    *

Does that hurt? Don't be a fool.
My finger-end blunders about
to close the wild eye of his sting.

Does that hurt? Don't be a fool.
It hurts as much as he knows,
but I tell him he's sure to live.

Does that hurt? Don't be a fool.
He flinches away with the pain
already a story: remember that bee?

Does that hurt? Don't be a fool.
He's off while the day we began with
still has some time left to run.

Does that hurt? Don't be a fool.
Just look at me watching him go
and you'd say I felt nothing at all.

Your Postcard Came

Your postcard came: a snap of Mediterranean blue
and bright chatter ending: How are you?

How am *I*? How are *you* is what I want to know –
last month checked over, stitched up, blasted with chemo

and now adrift, floating through days of slow sun
with one part of life finished, the next not yet begun.

And something else. I want to know too why the hell
last time you came to visit me at home I couldn't tell

how much better I might have made you feel
(no, 'loved', not 'better'; 'better' is too genteel)

if, instead of slipping out into the garden quietly
to pick the apples from our wet-leaved, sagging tree

– you said you felt like sleeping – I had just stayed close
and kept you talking. What came over me? Do I suppose

we'll always have enough time left for that?
That's shit.

The second I had propped
my ladder gingerly against the tree and crept

within its brittle globe – *hold tight! a child again!* –
and started rattling down the apple-rain,

I looked back at the house and found your face
inside the window like a silhouette in ice

and melting – skin becoming water and then air
before I stretched to pull the apples near,

the apples swelling air and water in their new-made skin.
How am I? I shall tell you, then.

I'm wishing you were here and well, that's all.
Not thinking how I climbed while you were waiting for the
fall.

Goethe in the Park

The slates have gone
from that shed in the park
where sometimes the old sat
if they were desperate,
and sometimes the young
with nowhere better to fuck,

and now given some luck
the whole piss-stinking thing
will fall to the ground,
no, I mean
will lift into space,
no evidence left

in its earthly place
of the grey graffiti runes,
the deck of glue,
the bench with broken ribs,
where if things had been different
I might have sat, or you.

This moral won't do.
Think of Goethe who
all those centuries back
found a pure space like that,
his bench an oak tree trunk,
his view

a plain of ripening wheat
where retriever-dog winds
in a clear track
raced forwards and back
laying a new idea at his feet
again and again,

again and again,
but not one the same,
until he was stuffed full
as one of those new-fangled air-balloons
and floated clear
into a different stratosphere.

The oak tree stayed,
its reliable trunk
making light of the sun,
its universe of leaves
returning just as they pleased
each spring, so life begun

was really life carried on,
or was
until a lightning bolt
drove hell-bent
through the iron bark
and split the oak in two.

This moral still won't do.
You see
one crooked piece of tree
broke free,

escaped the fire, and found its way
into the safe hands of a carpenter.

This man, he liked a shed.
(I should explain:
two hundred years have gone
since Goethe saw
the future run towards him
through the wide wheat plain.)

That's right; he liked a shed.
He liked the way a roof
could be a lid
and shut down heavily
to make a box,
a box which locked

so no one saw inside
the ranks
of gimcrack bunks,
or heard things said
by shapes that lay on them
with shaved heads,

not even him.
He just made what was ordered
good and sure,
saw everything was kept
the same, each nail,
each duckboard floor,

except, above one door
in pride of place

[137]

he carved his bit of tree,
not thinking twice,
into a face,
a merry gargoyle grimace.

This moral still won't do.
It's after dark,
and on my short-cut home to you
across the park
I smell the shed
before I see it: piss and glue

and something like bad pears,
and yet,
next thing I know
I've stepped inside it,
sat down on the bench
(it isn't pears, it's shit)

and stared up through
its rafters at the stars —
their dead and living lights
which all appear
the same to me,
and settle equally.

To Whom It May Concern

This poem about ice cream
has nothing to do with government,
with riot, with any political scheme.

It is a poem about ice cream. You see?
About how you might stroll into a shop
and ask: *One Strawberry Split. One Mivvi.*

What did I tell you? No one will die.
No licking tongues will melt like candle wax.
This is a poem about ice cream. Do not cry.

Tortoise

Here is a man who served his generals faithfully
and over the years had everything shot away
starting from the feet and working upwards:
feet, legs, chest, arms, neck, head.
In the end he was just a rusting helmet
on the lip of a trench. Then his chin-strap went.

So he became a sort of miraculous stone,
miraculous not just for the fine varnish
which shows every colour right to the depths –
black, topaz, yellow, white, grey, green –
but for the fact it can move. You see?
Four legs and a head and off he goes.

There's only one place to find the future now –
right under his nose – and no question either
where the next meal might be coming from:
jasmine, rose, cactus, marigold, iris, fuschia,
all snow their flowers round him constantly
and all in their different ways are so delicious.

It explains why there is no reason to hurry.
The breeze blows, the blossoms fall, and the head
shambles in and out as the mouth munches:
remorseless, tight, crinkled, silent, toothless, pink.
Life is not difficult any more, oh no; life is simple.
It makes you pause, doesn't it? It makes you think.

On the Table

I would like to make it clear that I have bought
this tablecloth with its simple repeating pattern
of dark purple blooms not named by any botanist
because it reminds me of that printed dress you had
the summer we met – a dress you have always said
I never told you I liked. Well I did, you know. I did.
I liked it a lot, whether you were inside it or not.

How did it slip so quietly out of our life?
I hate – I really hate – to think of some other bum
swinging those heavy flower-heads left to right.
I hate even more to think of it mouldering on a tip
or torn to shreds – a piece here wiping a dipstick,
a piece there tied round a crack in a lead pipe.

It's all a long time ago now, darling, a long time,
but tonight just like our first night here I am
with my head light in my hands and my glass full,
staring at the big drowsy petals until they start to swim,
loving them but wishing to lift them aside, unbutton them,
tear them, even, if that's what it takes to get through
to the beautiful, moon-white, warm, wanting skin of you.

Hey Nonny

I thought when the glass dropped and did not break
that the world I lived and breathed in was a fake,

and throwing the same glass out through a window
to hear it actually smash on the brick path below

didn't mean: *Oh, that's all right then, everything's OK,*
it meant thinking: *I see. Brilliant. In every possible way*

this fake is complete and perfect. Look at the stem —
a shattered icicle; look at the brim no longer a brim;

look at those two horny dogs which heard the crash
now swivelled apart, heads down and off in a rush.

That shows how complete and perfect. Everything just
a make-believe of itself. A dream. Nothing on trust.

Then I swivelled my own head a little. There was the world
caught as my glass had been caught, between held and
not-held:

the ash in my garden awake and bristled with spring,
its fistfuls of buds half-showing their soot-coloured wings;

new moss in the gutter; new haze of threadbare grass;
new crocus clumps plumping; new everything filled with the
grace

of life between nothing and something, filled with the sense
of learning again to belong, to be quickened by chance,

to be pitched once more through undoubtable air for the sake
of finding what next is in store, to fall, to see if I break.

Fresh Water

in memory of Ruth Haddon

I

This is a long time ago. I am visiting my brother, who is living
near Cirencester, and he says let's go and see the source of the
                                                            Thames.
It's winter. We leave early, before the sun has taken frost off
                                                        the fields,

and park in a lane. There's a painful hawthorn hedge with a
                                                            stile.
When we jump down, our boots gibber on the hard ground.
Then we're striding, kicking ice-dust off the grass to look
                                            confident —

because really we're not sure if we're allowed to be here.
In fact we're not even sure that this is the right place.
A friend of a friend has told us; it's all as vague as that.

In the centre of the field we find more hawthorn, a single
                                                        bush,
and water oozing out of a hole in the ground. I tell my brother
I've read about a statue that stands here, or rather lounges
                                                        here —

a naked, shaggy-haired god tilting an urn with one massive
                                                        hand.
Where is he? There's only the empty field glittering,
and a few dowager crows picking among the dock-clumps.

Where is Father Thames? My brother thinks he has been
                              vandalised
and dragged off by the fans of other rivers – they smashed the
                              old man's urn,
and sprayed his bare chest and legs with the names of rivals:

Trent, Severn, Nene, Humber. There's nothing else to do,
so I paddle through the shallow water surrounding the spring,
treading carefully to keep things in focus,

and stoop over the source as though I find it fascinating.
It is fascinating. A red-brown soft-lipped cleft
with bright green grass right up to the edge,

and the water twisting out like a rope of glass.
It pulses and shivers as it comes, then steadies
into the pool, then roughens again as it drains into the valley.

My brother and I are not twenty yet. We don't know who we
                              are,
or who we want to be. We stare at the spring, at each other,
and back at the spring again, saying nothing.

A pheasant is making its blatant *kok-kok*
from the wood running along the valley floor.
I stamp both feet and disappear in a cloud.

2

One March there's suddenly a day as warm as May, and my
                                                    friend
uncovers the punt he has bought as a wreck and restored,
cleans her, slides her into the Thames near Lechlade, and sets
                                                            off

upriver. Will I go with him? No, I can't.
But I'll meet him on the water meadows at the edge of town.
I turn out of the market square, past the church, and down
                                        the yew-tree walk.

Shelley visited here once – it's called Shelley's Walk –
but he was out of his element. Here everything is earth
and water, not fire and air. The ground is sleepy-haired

after winter, red berries and rain matted into it.
Where the yew-tree walk ends I go blind in the sun for a
                                                    moment,
then it's all right. There's the river beyond the boggy
                                            meadows,

hidden by reed-forests sprouting along its banks. They're
                                                    dead,
the reeds – a shambles of broken, broad, pale-brown leaves
and snapped bullrush heads. And there's my friend making

his slow curve towards me. The hills rise behind him
in a gradual wave, so that he seems at the centre
of an enormous amphitheatre. He is an emblem of something;

somebody acting something. The punt pole shoots up
wagging its beard of light, falls, and as he moves ahead
he leans forward, red-faced and concentrating.

He's expert but it's slow work. As I get closer I can hear
water pattering against the prow of the punt,
see him twisting the pole as he plucks it out of the gluey
river-bed.

I call to him and he stands straight, giving a wobbly wave.
We burst into laughter. He looks like a madman, floating
slowly
backwards now that he has stopped poling. I must look

like a madman too, mud-spattered and heavy-footed on the
bank,
wondering how I'm going to get on board without falling in.
As I push open the curtain of leaves to find a way,

I see the water for the first time, solid-seeming and mercury-
coloured.
Not like a familiar thing at all. Not looking
as though it could take us anywhere we wanted to go.

3

I've lived here for a while, and up to now the river has been
for pleasure. This evening people in diving suits have taken it
over.
Everyone else has been shooshed away into Christchurch
Meadow

or onto Folly Bridge like me. No one's complaining. The
summer evening
expands lazily, big purple and gold clouds building over the
Cumnor hills.
I have often stood here before. Away to the left you can see
Oxford

throwing its spires into the air, full of the conceited joy of
being itself.
Straight ahead the river runs calmly between boat-houses
before losing patience again, pulling a reed-shawl round its
ears,

snapping off willows and holding their scarified heads
underwater.
Now there's a small rowing boat, a kind of coracle below me,
and two policemen with their jackets off. The men shield
their eyes,

peering, and almost rock overboard, they're so surprised,
when bubbles erupt beside them and a diver bobs up –
just his head, streaming in its black wet-suit. There are
shouts –

See anything? – but the diver shrugs, and twirls his murky
torchlight
with an invisible hand. Everyone on the bridge stops talking.
We think we are about to be shown the story of the
river-bed –

its shopping trolleys and broken boat-parts, its lolling bottles,
its plastic, its dropped keys, its blubbery and bloated corpse.
But nothing happens. The diver taps his mask and disappears,

his fart-trail surging raucously for a moment, then subsiding.
The crowd in Christchurch Meadow starts to break up.
On Folly Bridge people begin talking again, and as someone
                                                    steps

off the pavement onto the road, a passing grocery van –
irritated by the press of people, and impatient with whatever
brought them together – gives a long wild *paarp* as it revs
                                                    away.

4

Now the children are old enough to see what there is to see
we take them to Tower Bridge and explain how the road lifts
                                                    up,
how traitors arrived at Traitor's Gate, how this was a
                                                    brewery

and that was a warehouse, how the river starts many miles
                                                    inland
and changes and grows, changes and grows, until it arrives
                                                    here,
London, where we live, then winds past Canary Wharf

(which they've done in school) and out to sea.
Afterwards we lean on the railings outside a café. It's autumn.
The water is speckled with leaves, and a complicated tangle
                                                    of junk

bumps against the embankment wall: a hank of bright grass,
a rotten bullrush stem, a fragment of dark polished wood.
One of the children asks if people drown in the river, and
                                                    I think

of Ruth, who was on the *Marchioness*. After her death, I met
someone who had survived. He had been in the lavatory when
the dredger hit,
and fumbled his way out along a flooded corridor, his shoes

and clothes miraculously slipping off him, so that when he at
last
burst into the air he felt that he was a baby again
and knew nothing, was unable to help himself, aghast.

I touch my wife's arm and the children gather round us.
We are the picture of a family on an outing. I love it. I love the
river
and the perky tour-boats with their banal chat. I love the snub
barges.

I love the whole dazzling cross-hatchery of traffic and
currents,
shadows and sun, standing still and moving forward.
The tangle of junk bumps the wall below me again and I look
down.

There is Ruth swimming back upstream, her red velvet party
dress
flickering round her heels as she twists through the locks
and dreams round the slow curves, slithering on for miles

until she has passed the ponderous diver at Folly Bridge
and the reed-forests at Lechlade, accelerating beneath bridges
and willow branches,
slinking easily among the plastic wrecks and weedy trolleys,

speeding and shrinking and silvering until finally she is sliding
                                                          uphill
over bright green grass and into the small wet mouth of the
                                                          earth,
where she vanishes.

YORK NOTES

General Editors: Professor A.N. Jeffares (*University*

YORK PRESS
Immeuble Esseily, Place Riad Solh, Beirut.

LONGMAN GROUP UK LIMITED
Longman House, Burnt Mill, Harlow,
Essex CM20 2JE, England
Associated companies, branches and representatives
throughout the world

First published 1986
Sixth impression 1993

ISBN 0-582-79222-3

Produced by Longman Singapore Publishers Pte Ltd
Printed in Singapore